you

Tulika Kirtiman

BookLeaf Publishing

India | USA | UK

Presentation by *BookLeaf Publishing*

Web: www.bookleafpub.com

E-mail: info@bookleafpub.com

ISBN: 9789363310711

First edition 2024

Perfection

Beware of me!
I march into lives,
An unparalleled light,
And as is fate, I leave,
A sea of blight behind.

I have seen all there is to see,
Been wherever one could be,
On the wings of my mind,
And countless horses in my eyes.

Painstakingly have I sculpted,
Me in the image of purity,
Divine, it gleams and freezes,
Earthly seasons and passions alight.

My skin perfumes the ether,
But none have come near,
To sully these wafting gossamers,
Of my breath and my words.

Ages and seasons touched me,
My scintillating being thusly,
Has become impervious to charms,
And quick to repel curious chisels.

I am the sculpture by the seas,
Proudly weathering its acridity,
Its lashing all frozen to steam,
Slowly shrouding me in mysteries…

My Voice

So many voices within me,
And I do not know how to speak.

Each voice embracing,
Every fibre of my being.

I have yet to learn,
How to corral multiple desires.

And I silently watch them,
Singing odes to my visions.

Silence is the key, I see,
It cuts through the chaos.

Opening a vault deep within,
Where hums my heart.

Cradling the sweet hum,
I join the melee with glee.

Now my sentinels are here,
Ready to scour the ether for You…

The hum that cuts me.

Something to say

Have you got something to say?
Your eyes have been screaming,
All day all night,
In consternation, maybe?

Have you got something to say?
Your lips have been biting,
In the air all around,
Begging for music, maybe?

Have you got something to say?
Your fingers have been singing,
Lullabies all along,
On the prowl for secrets, maybe?

Have you got something to say?
You have been sleepily running,
From me since the beginning,
Searching for anchors in worlds keening,
maybe?

Yours, until…

I come from the suns' fires,
Do not mistake me for moons.

I am Yours in mind, body, soul,
Until You use me to sow discord.

My hands are solely for Your care,
Not to violently smear nature's birth.

My fires burn for me to warm You,
So do not depend on conflagrations to stave ruin.

My mind forges worlds on my breath,
So never come to cease another's breaths.

My songs and my colours are born from joy,
Never can angry disdain flow from them.

My steps are my children from rhythm,
Unbridled shall they be from ageing.

My eyes pierce veils for me to decorate,
So do not seek salvation in their depths.

For I carry forgotten, maybe missed,

Devils, harbouring their powers to love You.

So my Love, forgive this devil, will You?

Finding my story

Lying strewn on the edge,
Of my touch and skin,
Lurking just around the corner,
On the tip of my tongue and ears.

In the midst of this melee,
My mind conjures rendezvous,
Bleary enough to let breathe,
My recklessly adamant hope.

To my heart this cacophony,
Is a time of delightful,
Creation of dreams and needs,
Far beyond the horizons of sanity.

Even my tears forced out,
My eyes, feast on this spectacle,
Somehow merging all sought and,
Beyond, into a starry tapestry.

Will I find who calls me?
A new language perhaps to see,
What has eluded me always,
On the delicious brink of reality.

Fearing silences

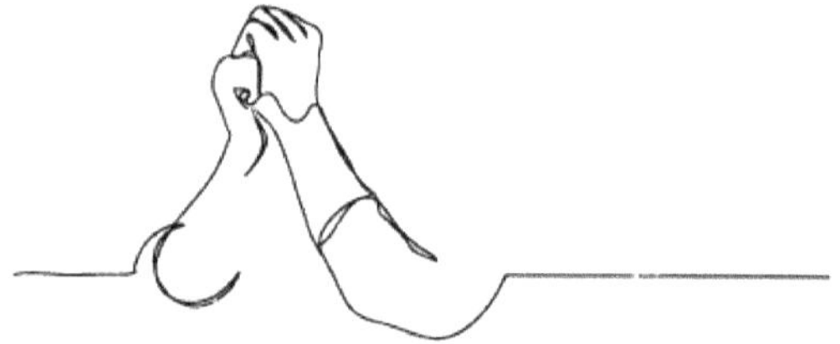

Silences have never been,
My strength, for they open me,
To my wildfires that were lit,
Long ago by hands now condemned.

Screams I thought were silenced,
Begin to ring in the corridors,
Of my heart, barely clenching to
Reason, as my mind cleaves.

It is these very fault lines,
That Your fortuitous floods meet,
As they crowd me wholly in warmth,
That sadly is still too new, still too far.

But rest assured, my only Love,
Your warmth will be home tomorrow,
In me, right where I am bloodied,
Today, that tomorrow is right about now.

And then our silences shall,
Incense our mischief and peace,
Building anticipation for endless creations,
In paints, in ink, also throaty and rhythmic.

Seeking Your spells

My spirit yearning for the primal truth of love,
Gave freely, speck by speck, flame by flame,
Lit up paths for the damned and blessed alike,
To its regal slavery mocking the untamed.

Conflagrations unerringly burning out cold,
Trudging on drab sibilant sands all alone,
My frantic fingers fall frozen against time,
Scouring all my fields for weeds to atone.

Eyes trained on their placid, unyielding wool,
A patchwork of smoky smiles and languid lies,
Sheltering me from the raucous titanic radiance,
Of fires scalding the tears that my smile belies.

Leaden body lying weightless in empty spaces,
Replete with sighs and silent cries for mercy,
With seasons rolling on my feet pulling me
apart,
From the essence of life, definitely, tersely.

My silent voice hoarse with prayers and spite,
Vindictively slashes at foggy fiendish struggles,
Of apoplectic apathy for my bottomless heart,
And sneering misty walls refusing to buckle.

Thus shorn of the deep warmth of love,
Its boisterous cocoons full of downy swells,
Of whispers and glances probing lips and skin,
Whose touch I crave in their comely spells.

Broken for You

A pretty sculpture I make,
Impervious to tears and smiles,
Proudly have I fought time,
While withering deep within.

My eyes touch only the Perfect,
Tinged with my fortress's march to,
Staccato strains wrought,
In my proud scaffoldings.

I stand in the sky,
Safe from the seasons,
As the suns and thunders,
Weep and rip me slowly within.

Immune in my drunken stupor,
I traverse the azure, all alone,
Wishing for a nameless face,
A familiar warmth.

Bleeding,
Tearing,
Breaking me…

Pain deep within

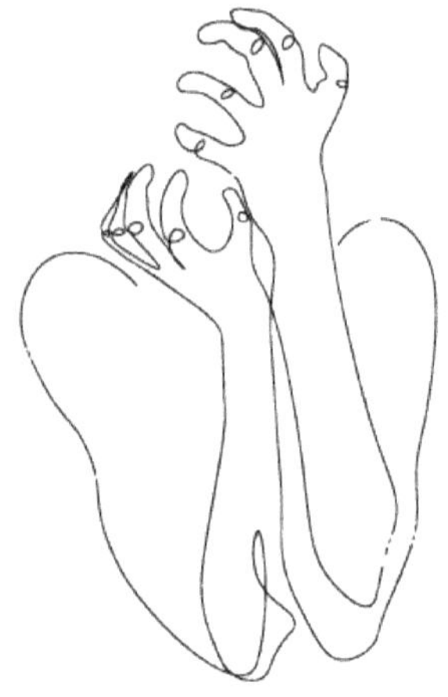

Why give me a heart,
When there is nothing,
To fill it except my,
Empty ruby blood?

Why pour this love in me,
When my body is already,
Burning with each heartbeat,
Barely able to contain it?

Why make my soul sing,
Songs that rip my burns,
Bathing me in ambrosial tears,
And bleeding lights?

Why scald me with passions,
So great that my mind,
Takes me to a world,
Where all I see is You?

Why give me eyes,
That see beyond my,
Singing pain and anoint,
You with my scents?

Why give me questions,
When smiles are the only answer,
I dearly resent,
And deeply cherish?

Not enough

Is it not enough?
I wonder often,
My back bearing the brunt.

The blood trickling tickles my skin,
Making me laugh unabashedly,
At the caution I took always.

The steely pull of the ichor,
Drags me to a new reality,
Where my mind goes into free fall.

A sea of sensations greets me,
A beach of grainy emotions meets me,
As the thudding panic of my heart beats me.

Somehow I want to rest here,
Lay all my prejudices bare,
Anything to make it easier to bear…

The insistent pull of reality,
To heal the back finally,
So I can look forward to finalities.

Wither

Many things,
Like people are meant,
To wither away.

It is not love,
To make them prosper,
When they are long gone.

They must go,
To create the tinder,
For the future we need.

Life is finite,
So the earth must,
Gorge on the past.

Then the flames,
From its belly,
Will touch the skies.

Colouring it peacefully,
With endless hope and strength.

Idyllic Ironies

In my eyes float,
Memories of a past,
Yet to come.

My throat bubbles forth,
With mirth of unseen times,
At words yet unheard.

In my ears ring,
Mellifluous rustling of leaves,
On paths uncharted.

I wonder what these,
Echoes are, memories unmade,
Of a world on whose edge I am.

When my heart is bursting,
Why do my hands grow emptier?

When I can see You,
Why can I not grasp You?

When I am senseless already,
Right here in this world,
When shall I lose my mind,
To finally reach You?

Hope realised

My veins bloom and roar with sweet infernos,
Insomnolent limbs climb out of their winters,
My breath merrily calls out to howling gales,
Cleaving all of my ignorance to splinters.

My eyes set the sun ablaze through the dawn,
Ripping birdsongs and colours apart to words,
They behold the deific coiled thunderbolt,
Who sundered my being from the curse.

Lying deep in the golden thalassic belly,
My mellifluous heart rises to the songs,
Of sempiternal longing within my soul,
Where His piercing love always belongs.

His love etches deep beyond my bones,
Lancing through my breathy deeds and haze,
In the cerulean mere of my grateful soul,
Where I shelter His pearl in my lotus, unfazed.

Seeking Me

In exuberant forests bursting with hues whirling,
How will You find me as we twirl amongst
trees?
So let me leave flecks of me penetrating the
throng,
To reach out and help You find Your way back
to me.

My lips are flowers hiding unalloyed ferocity,
And my gentle hands are capable of plunder,
My touch is the balmy sands sheltering
treasures,
My tender being fires up to tear my malice
asunder.

Soaking Your keen ears, my wings zip past
foliage,
Perfuming dull forests with my rhythm and
streak,
Happily pillaging restive streams and boughs,
A fleck will rip still skies with my fiery spree.

Lunging laughter to pierce every little breath,
My joviality You will find in the macabre and
serene,

My eyes are the midnight pools of potent
silence,
That cradle the unsaid behind hooded screens.

Finally, the flecks will be in the songs in my
heart,
That forged letters and colours to bejewel You,
While my soul dances to dark eccentric
cadences,
My astute calm will envelop and welcome You.

Seeking You

Amongst stars studded, I will see Your puissant
soul,
Holding thundering reins of the inventive Sun,
Bestowing upon me the lavishness of Your hunt
for,
My rainstorms that hold ice and fires as one.

You, who I have sought in faces and voices
around,
Leaving me high and dry, hungering after only
You,
I will find You in the light dusting Your
heartstrings,
That whisper to me to open my eyes and hold
You.

I will look into the suns of Your irradiant eyes,
Led by the me I lost to You in the past,
A proud scar today, it bears Your bold marks,
In my soul and heart till eternity lasts.

I will seek Your touch clawing at my chaos
within,
Seeping as answers against veils of the
unknown,

Your untamed effulgence will be my great
fortune,
To which I will be led by my bold heart alone.

My heart will roar with crystal chimes in my
ribs,
Of long-held dreams bursting through strife,
And Your perfumes will cull my timorous
illusions,
For Your legions of suns to bloom in my life.

Knowing You

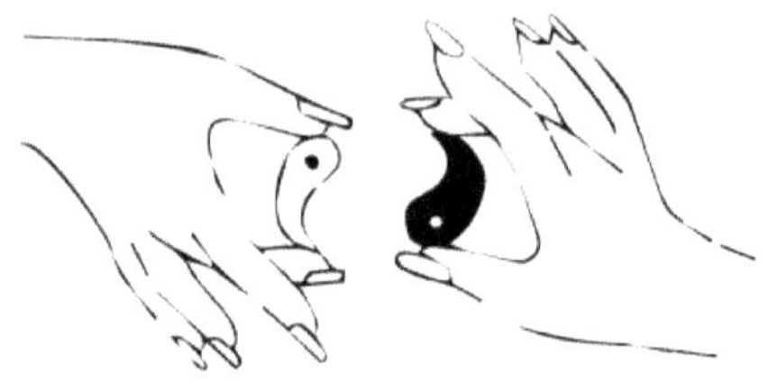

Nice to meet You, my Love,
We have never met,
And I do know You still,
From my dreams' edge.

Where I held You,
Not in my arms as a lullaby,
Not in my eyes as a sigh,
Not on my lips as a wish.

Rather I have,
Pulled You in through smiles,
Wrapped You in my scents,
Cherished You in my movements.

So even though I have,
Yet to know Your name,
Yet to call Your face,
Yet to feel Your embrace.

I know You,
Living in the echoes,
Of my being,
Calling out to me.

Preparations

I silently wrestle with Fate,
So that my fires never dim,
In the worst of calms.

I sit amongst my flowers,
So that my fragrance,
Never deserts me in storms.

I run with the winds,
So that my dainty feet,
Never hesitate to follow You.

I burn away with fires,
So that my heart,
Does not give up in Your dark.

I lie down in the snow,
So that my body,
Never shies away from loneliness.

I look at the sun,
In its countless eyes,
So I can bear You in mine.

Many worlds within me

Out of the many worlds within me,
I wonder which would You choose first.

They all breathe for You,
A new world on each breath,
I wonder which ones would You breathe.

Each world is an unnamed,
Colour, staining my blood,
I wonder which colours shall immerse You.

Countless strains of melodies,
Are the footsteps in my bones,
I wonder which songs will sing You.

Innumerable lights dance away,
Warming the beats of my heart,
I wonder which warmth shall covet You.

Amongst these brimming worlds,
I wonder which one will be captured by You…

Finally under Your spell

Jocular thunderbolts cutting through skies,
Bleeding famished light onto terrene platters,
They go cleaving evasive sands and smoke,
Wresting perfidious glares for rains to shatter.

Raindrops grinding interminable winters,
That bested my aestival soul of whirling fires,
They lacerate my torpidity and open my soul,
To lofty grounds held up by my dreams' spires.

My body reposes under skies that never left me,
Drenching in lavish squalls of warmth and light,
Cradling this dithering ignoramus of my heart,
That no longer strays from His caresses slight.

I slowly rise to life with meres ripping marshes,
Body thrumming in its sapphire with susurrant
ichor,
My mind falls asleep, urged by His argent
breath,
So my heart can wash its sorrows with petrichor.

Cast on my hapless heart's scorned ardour,
Was a spell I sought for my apathy to be quelled,
To melt away fear and dubiety and give way to
love,
To drag me to His paradise, raising me out of my
hell.

Birth of a warrior

Along the paths we hewed through,
Sometimes I think as I stand alone,
Why does my heart scream for You,
Stirring up restless fires in my bones?

Was it wrong to drink the aether,
Yearning for the drizzle of Your winds?
Did my veins burn my corrugated life,
To let Your suns amble on my skin?

You lovingly stoked my undying heart,
By Your answer that this is all mine,
For wings soar only when tinged in pain,
As the price for our resolve to shine.

So I laugh with my bleeding warrior,
Feeding fires to rob endless nights,
While I claim my destiny from them,
My warrior smiles within my light.

The weight of love

Being by Your side forever shall be,
The most welcome weight on my shoulders,
Consuming eternal devotion as Your birthright,
It shakes me free of unwelcome boulders.

Clutching my backbone with calloused fingers,
Their chains on my soul thus ascended,
To macerate my scapulae with dystopias,
Of leaden wings leaving the skies upended.

Your love is the weight that cut me free,
Taking over every smidgen of my being,
Filling me with the artistry of Your soul,
Leaving me in its gardens and trees.

My garden awaits You in Your soul,
An anchor for You in the waltzing melee,
All my wishes and Yours in its trees,
It proudly floats on the edge of sanity.

My Love

Churning seas of my soul dyed with hope,
His fathomless, unforgiving love blooms,
Scars and fears now proudly guide Him to,
My sanctum sanctorum tinged by His perfumes.

The soft iridescence of His rufescent love,
Washes me in the hues of thalassic calm,
Swimming in its fortunes is a rare honour,
Relieving me of egotistic embers in my palms.

Beyond desperate tirades of reprobates,
While stony unbelievers seek an escape,
His tyrannical rains of relentless love,
Leads my sorrowful prejudices astray.

His delicate love feeds my daunting warmth,
And enlightens me with His powers sublime,
Moving worlds and hearts to its sacred law,
It daringly strides in the face of Time.

His love never owned is wise and wild,
A beauty unexampled eternally it remains,
A myth for my warring heart and anima,
That He slew to immortality free from taint.

His Love

My nascent heart wakes to dawns of reality,
My surrender to You, raging in its depths,
Blossoming gossamer tears to finally unveil,
Our new world through which my feet swept.

Here my being colossal and unconquered,
Will be Your haven against whirlwinds of Time,
Each heartbeat holds a world within,
So You never see unknown roads or climes.

In my smiles and laughter lie homes for You,
Encompassing Your vast dreams befitting,
Your titanic being that nature gloats over,
Adorned with the majestic as well as flitting.

In prayers for You, I will make all of You mine,
From Your ambrosial jubilance and pride,
To Your comets of fears, sorrows, and wrath,
And piercing doubts that You lovingly hide.

Every fibre of my being welcomes us,
To swathe You in my words, colours, scent,
That lie beyond needs fulfilled on my own,
As my Desire that can never be spent.

With my firestorm spirit soaked with our desires,
I will take You to untouched skies of Your soul,
To forever protect You and Your magnificence,
I will realise my Desire and never let go.

His Pearl heart

Your pearl in my palm,
A flaming flower that sailed on azure tides,
I look on wondering what all does it hide,
In its proud, thrumming strides.

Within Your pearl,
Do specks of Your stentorian words twirl?
Does Your gaze beckon storms to swirl?
Does Your touch grace its gossamer whorls?

Does Your pearl,
Cradle Your supple breaths laced with calm,
Contain Your embrace of many fathoms,
Cherish Your lips with my name, a psalm?

Does Your pearl,
Hold Your dreams for our lives to merrily tend,
To my nights with jewels of Your warm rents,
Quenching my fires with Your lofty scent?

Your pearl mirthfully,
Answered my arrows with gentleness,
That conjured clouds wispy and dense,
Quashed the pacing of my heart senseless.

Your pearl heart thus,
Soothed undercurrents flooding the waves,
With my tenacity that has the way paved,
To freely amble in all the joys we create.

My lotus garden

As I swam in the lakes of Your paradise,
Bathed with my diamantine bouquets,
My lazed strokes etch my love in them,
And lotus pods of hopes for You to regale.

I see You cut the waters seeking them,
Unfurling them with Your gaze keen,
Letting go of the breath of heavens,
They held for You in their eyes serene.

My breath slides on their silky petals,
Their dewdrops house my scintillant eyes,
Your sorrows on sepals shall wither,
In peduncles rises the covenant of our ties.

To swathe Your paradise with my prayers,
Their colours beckon curious winds,
I hold You safe within the eternal sheen,
Of Your lakes marked with my diamonds.

So freely partake of my lotus garden,
Drenched by hues of Your divine rains,
Adorned with laughter from Your suns,
All silenced at nights in Your embrace.

My heart is Yours

Today my heart of unnumbered rooms,
Resplendent with my songs to be born,
Lights its passageways for You,
With ferocious love like a sunny morn.

Million strings harping rich strains,
Pulling Your suns for a dance in halls,
Floors tremble in their caressing snares,
While roofs sway and smile enthralled.

Walls thrum with notches and scars,
From stories of wrongs too costly,
They are windows today You slip in,
To claim me in Your palaces hoary.

In my heart that never can be tamed,
My treasures finally find their way,
Forever Yours to rule and exult in,
As You own them by Your ardent gaze.

Keeper of my heart

I awaited my claim to what's already mine,
To efface my longstanding agony,
So smiles borne of my heart can slice,
Silent pasts from today's symphony.

My bosom surges with Your lifeblood,
Claiming its pedestal of Your arms,
Erasing all that had it enervated,
In the pits of Your fiery charms.

This is where Your abode stands,
Fragrant with drifts of Your deluge,
Of murmuring moonlights peopled,
By Your touch holding my refuge.

Your scalding breaths stud my heart,
To watch over our world within,
So no longer shall any soul waltz in,
And drive my love to wear itself thin.

Drunk on You

How did You live in my verses?
How did You shiver my perennial calm?
How did Your arrows decorate my breaths?
How did You marshal a heart becalmed?

I sense the savagery of Your love,
Pulling my spirit to the music of Manea,
Its sonorous answers sound the knell,
To arid ease reigning my sweet mania.

I will unchain Your passion with my eyes,
With sensations You can never transcend,
I will feed on the emotions off Your skin,
Leaving You burning in fires without end.

Rid of cloying twines of vacillation,
Unperturbed by nights under Your wings,
I will perfect the rapture of loving You,
Till my name and scent rule my king.

When can I see You?

I long to see You,
Free from my dreary dreams,
What can I do now that I want You?

I want to see You,
Would You not spare some mercy,
For me enthralled and harried by You?

I want to see You,
Each breath burning my calm away,
Because my fires have begun to betray.

I want to see You,
So I can finally put a face,
To the peace that comes from You.

I want to see You,
In me, who lives only for You,
And seeks my sun to outshine me.

I want to see You,
So come home to shatter me,
As I await You finding Your way to me.

Love amidst trade

I am a merchant of words and colours,
Of the rushing purpose, faces, sighs,
Where my prismatic-blooded brushes,
Soothe hearts with joys earlier denied.

My mind rains down on my hands,
Weaving tapestries from my heart,
While legacies and curses within,
Chase the damned for my reward.

I am exacting with destinies,
That seek in me a final place to rest,
Far away from their demanding ties,
I treasure You in my breast.

Freeing us

I tried to hide You,
Curtained by my eyelids,
Held within my fingers,
Fears lacing its derisory lattice.

My heart tried to contain You,
On its throne, and rooms plenty,
My mind baffled by Your magic,
Has battled Your grace aplenty.

Your laugh breaks the impasse,
Helping me battle with myself,
A laugh thus breaking from me,
Quenching the folly of my quest.

At last I lost myself to You,
Beyond every dual existence,
I find myself in Your swells,
Basking in You, my deliverance.

A heart made of love

With tempests in my heart now calm,
I behold its crystalline streaks,
Prodding its lakes with new eyes,
We urge the past to speak.

Ready to give up on love,
Stung in the deepest parts,
My heart fought back hopelessly,
Against the lure of life's darts.

Nowhere to hide with walls crumbling,
Unaware of the life rushing in,
Every draft of air became my heart's,
Cherishing those on wrong roads taken.

Becoming Me I dreamt of incessantly,
Alive like never before my heart leaps,
No longer I shall hide from our love,
Born of rivers that wash away our satiety.

Through me

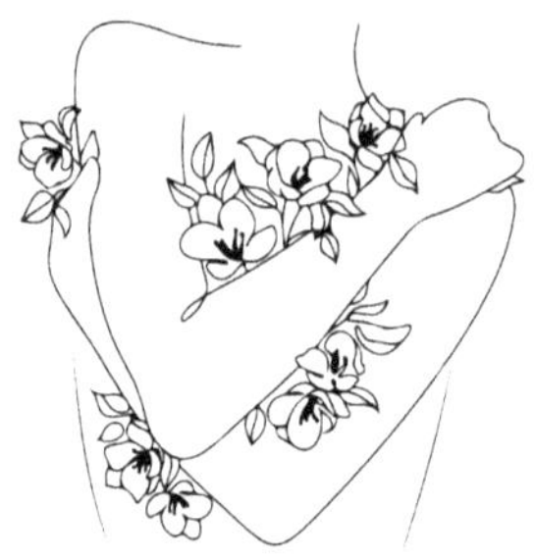

I want You to feel me,
With every fibre of Your being,
For it is You that is housed in me.

Have You never wanted to see,
How You are feeling inside of me?

Have Your eyes never thirsted,
To know how You see through me?

Has Your voice never rushed forth,
To sing the songs You find within me?

Has Your blood never sung to You,
To know how mine burns and swirls in me?

Tell me, O my dearest, have You never,
Known that this body of mine,
Has come from You to me?

Absent

I am absent from the world,
People ask me where I am.

I smile and twinkle my eyes,
Urging the words through sighs.

From the mythical border,
Of dreams where,
Reality is created.

It is the forge where fates,
Are fought for and written,
By the brute of our souls.

It is here that I find You,
Finally after searching,
The wrong world for ages.

It is here that I finally,
Call my home as I,
Smile and sigh at the world passing by…

Absent from the world.

At the market

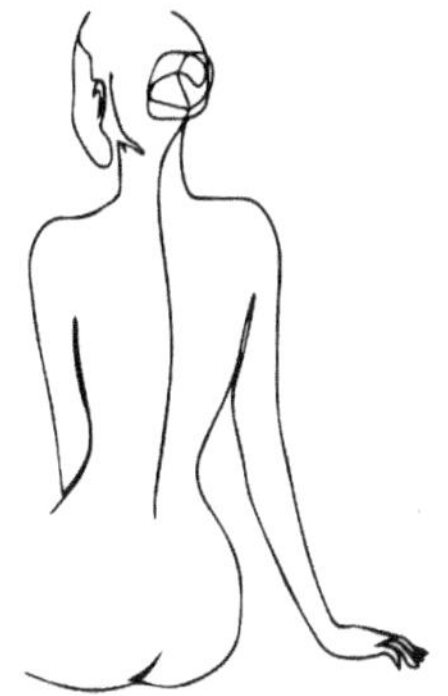

I stand in the Market,
Wondering how much I cost.

My wares are as rare as smiles,
In a world ripped by solitude.

My wares are invaluable,
For I deal with a currency,
Made just for me.

Minted in my name alone,
They are forged in a kiln,
Bellowing my name.

Eyes that can contain me,
Arms that can understand me,
A being that can buy me.

That is the Buyer I await,
That is His voice beckoning me,
To steady my wares.

Barely patient, I silently watch,
The world sails in His seas,
As I prepare to be bought,
To hell or heaven,
Maybe both…

Waiting for You

I have been waiting for You,
Cradled in the jubilant mantle rent,
Of dancing nights and their phantasmic din,
The stars gnashing dubiety of aeons pent.

I have been waiting for You,
In the statuesque Sun's effulgent display,
Of aureate gentleness and ebullience,
Rending my adamantine apathy away.

I have been waiting for You,
Meandering through choppy moonlights,
Setting the slumbering world at large aflame,
Hungrily lapping up my dismissive sighs.

I have been waiting for You,
Drunk on persistent zephyrs that lashed,
My volatile spirit with ambrosia and incense,
Gifts from heavens seeping into my flesh.

I have been waiting for You,
In beds of oceanic raindrops' gleam,
Each holding a world as they righteously slid,
Enlivening my parched, cloistered dreams.

I have been waiting for You,
Swathed in the embrace of bows and ties,
Peppered with songs of souls and birds,
And my desires in infinite cloaks of my skies.

I have been waiting for You,
Holding You close in my bated breath,
As I sought my place in this wispy world,
And ours on the crowded horizon's breadth.

Bloodied feet

Akin to canaries bursting as,
Fiery songs from gilded cages,
My lips let out silent shrieks,
In tongues no mind could comprehend.

Rushing with knowing currents,
Of the air and the seas,
The jagged rocks cleanse,
Old skin and blood off my feet.

Painting the sands sanguine,
And the breeze in mighty flares,
I want to grasp this new feeling,
That knocked down my confused glare.

There really is nothing,
To understand or see,
All of it has already been,
Deep within me for centuries.

Though it is here I lost,
My ties to all that has been,
So I could sail unbounded without,
Arms or mind desperate to reach.

To race to reach past horizons,
Has lost all meaning for me,
I have nowhere left to reach anymore,
For I met destiny on my bloodied feet…

Losing my mind

Opening my clenched eyes,
Letting go of my set palms,
I set my crumbling marble cage,
On blistering sands.

Its veins pristine,
Feed the sands and the seas,
While I am blissful,
In a new body, a new being.

Sights and songs come,
Rushing to me on His waves,
Without my sentinel mind,
I know now all that is to come.

My heart is sonorous here,
Seasons long held sprout,
Through every pore, my feet,
Hurry on rocks unhurt.

Without a care for worlds,
Or an errant thought I wonder,
Is it possible to be this ecstatic?

Have I really become free?

Smithereens

Wintry eyes of mine,
Regard the world,
With a plea to dash me,
To smithereens.

It is a time like any other,
My breath has remained the same,
Then why do the seas,
Suddenly charge at me?

Rooted in my pedestal, I see a wave,
Gentle and gigantic, it rolls lazily,
Adamant on pulling me down,
It pushes me into its dark vortices.

There, old and new worlds,
The present and the past,
All make sense and none,
To my finally silent heart.

In this dance of vortices,
Swirl many deaths for me,
Losing the last of my ethereal roots,
I lie broken on the rocks…

Finally free.

Found my words

Waking up to my present and past,
I have found my story at last.

Let me tell You what,
I see, has always been,
In the very world I breathed,
My last, stands the new unseen.

Do not ask me how,
It came to be or how,
Do I see the things,
That I now see.

The price I realise,
For this new tongue is,
My long sought restraint,
And the supreme shield of reality.

Defenceless and carefree thus,
I stand battered by arrows,
Tipped with lotuses and roses,
And dewy barbs of the laughing morn.

Eyes wet with its dew,
Arms encumbered with boughs,
I am to only move with my earth,
And blissfully write new storms…

Truly free

Everywhere I turn to look,
My broken perfection I find,
Asleep, peacefully asunder.

Never could my heart know,
The feeling of deliverance,
Bleeding and sweating through,
Imperfections deeper than my skin.

My visage crackling to smoke,
Smiles erupt from fires deepset,
A new weightlessness weighs me,
Down, right to my soul.

Rid of my perversions,
Coiling my gullible heart,
Alien sensations familiar,
Reside in my awestruck heart.

I am free, truly…

Immortal

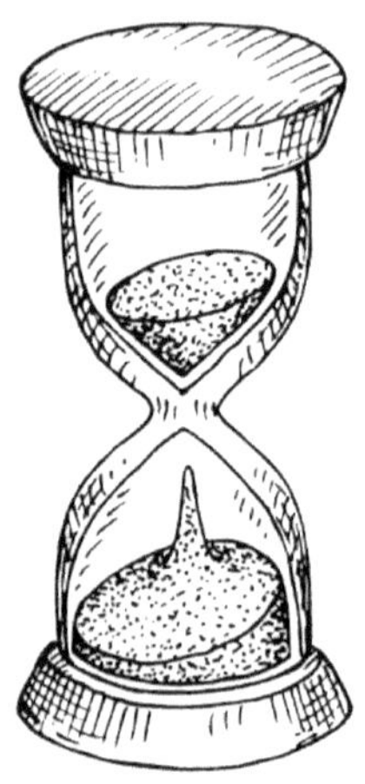

In my new body,
Tasting with my new tongue,
I do not want to give up,
On my immortality.

In the throes of paradise,
I have already given my all,
So I can fly higher and farther,
On the countless breezes for me.

Shattering my castles,
Withering my humbled sentinels,
I have reached Your hand,
Right on the bridge of Time.

Timelessness is a taste,
I have found indescribably sweet,
You are what it held,
All along in my streets from me.

So tell me why should I,
Die and melt away to nothingness,
When lifetimes are insignificant,
To devote to You and my wishes?

Reality crashing in

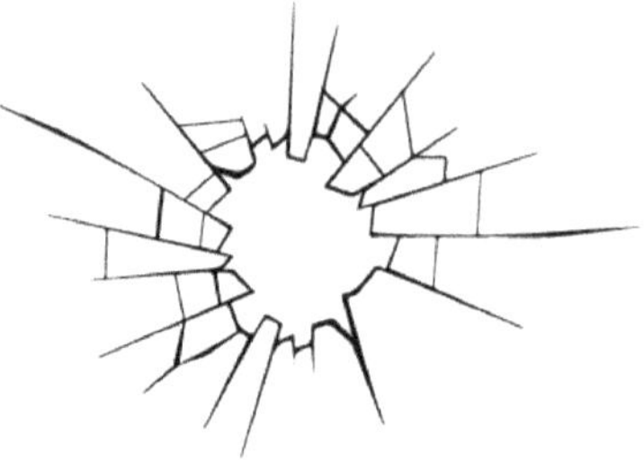

On the sweet foam,
Sails my dream of paradise,
I wave it hearty farewells,
From my tempestuous cliffs.

Now I have entered the world,
Of endings and beginnings,
Quick as blinks and sure as sighs,
Unmarred by the staff of Time.

These rocks that nurse on my
Blood, have healed my feet,
Crisp sheets of breezes have,
Enlivened my marble being.

Now, now I do see You!
You, who has taken apart,
My mists, to create fables,
From a new world for me.

Now, now I can feel You,
Better than the most potent dreams,
A form which nobody can replicate,
I finally have the eyes to replete endlessly.

When You came

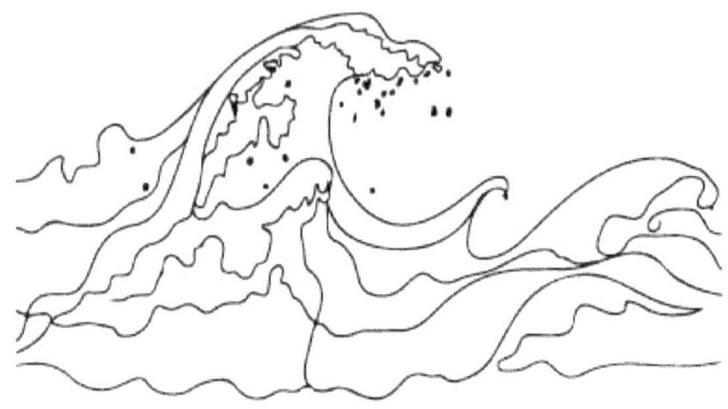

The very first moments,
Of meeting You shall be with me,
As a start of a new life for me.

It was under the loving blanket,
Of Nyx with her innumerable eyes,
That I lost my composure at last.

Indeed, Chaos ruled that day,
For all my old ways gathered dust,
Steadily, leaving me stunned in Your light.

Unearthing me from my ruins,
I never could believe I was healing,
Growing, a fire of pelagic proportions.

Weightless shoulders and an empty mind,
I was rather carried away by You,

Instead of flying while carrying You.

Thus my bones unknew their burdens,
And my smiles did not hurt me at all,
I knew at once it obviously made sense.

My fortuitous destiny carrying Your name,
Had finally come to drown me in lavish
waves…

Alive again

Invigorated by my roars,
I have awoken to newness,
That I have known already,
Deep down in my bones and soul.

Spent all night talking,
To the moon and her curious stars,
Who ushered You ceremoniously,
So my eyes would never close for You.

The night melded deliciously,
Into the garrulous arms of dawn,
Its chatter finally put me,
To reluctant sleep begrudging its cheer.

Tell me, O Sun,
What did the dawn whisper,
Into His gentle ears,
Was it an entreaty that I could fulfil?

You know I have never been this alive,
Can I hold onto my life,
With so much vitality and purpose,
Flooding my crazed dancing veins.

I see now that only living with You,
Shall be my ruthless solace…

What do I do?

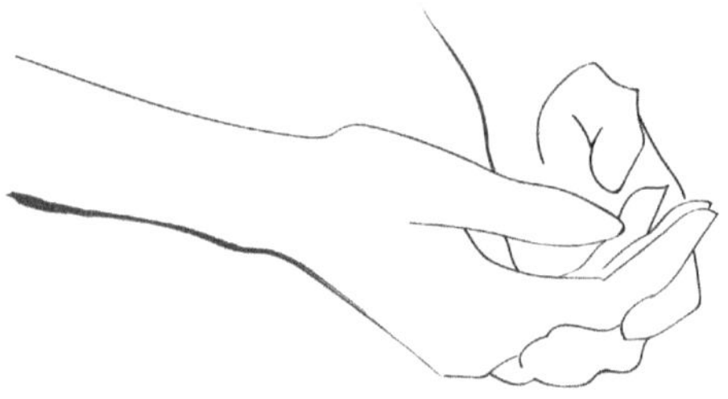

What do I do,
Now that I have seen You?

With the calm of calamities,
Gone in a heartbeat,
What do I do,
Now that I am so happy?

My heart beats no longer,
Flowing insanely in Time,
What do I do,
Now bereft of choppy seas?

My mind is brimming,
And empty simultaneously,
What do I do,
Now free from pristine sanity?

My soul is sated at last,

Running in our meadows,
What do I do,
Now without a stitch of order?

I stand before You

I stand before You.
Yearning, rushing through our eyes,
Shields abating our powers for us,
That we let go through our eyes.

I stand before You.
Gleefully bared by our eyes intense,
Our hearts brawl to leap out,
To pull us to our destiny intent.

I stand before You.
Minds milling in hazes of existence,
Our prowling breaths of billowing fires,
Bathing everything old in our scent.

I stand before You.
Our bodies strummed by zephyrs,
Fanning flames coiled unbeknownst,
Seeking our fires to quench these fires.

I stand before You.
Our bodies long melted to ether,
Raving to live our whimsical destiny,
Shaky bodies losing loss as their tether.

I stand before You.
Old worlds toppling over precipices,
Hungrily seeking us to mark as ours,
Every sensation bolstered in our lattice.

I stand before You.
Scarred by love on our eager skin,
Time halts its unforgiving march for us,
So we may burn in our paradise of few blinks.

You heard me

Deafened by lugubrious doldrums,
My spirit wrestled against invisible shackles,
Even free from its marble bosom.

Losing my mind, I thought, would ease me,
But my empty canvas now howled,
Tearing my silence to bloodied thirst.

Drenched in Your ambrosial grace,
My ears thrash my languorous being,
To quench the shy drought within.

Not once, not twice, but all night,
You heard me warbling as a songbird,
Of its travails and hopes hungrily.

Too scared to lose this kindred spirit,
My shy wings glazed off of You,
So You stay here with me and take in sail.

Then, at complete ease, You can find,
Your peace at last under my wings,
Just as I sang finally under Your sails.

Leap of faith

You, who rode the tempests majestically,
Do You really want me?

I saw Your waves recede, drawing my tears,
Was that so You could gather,
A mighty army of will and want,
To spark Your raging fire in me?

My whole being urges me on,
My heart is pushing me off the cliff,
My mind is rattling with clouds,
My feet rooted in quiet desperation.

Then I raise my unfazed eyes,
To meet Your soul shining in Yours,
And it is at that instant I knew,
That I have ceased to be.

Your unspoken pain calling for me,
Your hands outstretched for my wings,
Your waves commence the ritual of death,
For my closure to be able to be Yours.

A single tower of water rises,
Tinged in Your scent and voice,
It crashes at my feet patiently,
As my faith in You makes me gleefully leap…

Chasing me

Let go of the inferno within You,
Into ruddy seas to melt all scars,
Against maddeningly slow nights,
So You can paint me in Your stars.

I have begun to feel the billowing,
Seas of ours below and above,
In whose delirious flames,
I have finally sought Your love.

Come trap me in Your breaths,
And wrestle me into bliss without haste,
Stripping my delicacy and nescience,
To feast in deliverance of Your chase.

His Footsteps

In my blurry dreams,
Now of an age and life long gone,
I do recall footsteps of destiny resounding.

But my new being clearly,
Never even heard You coming,
Let alone recognize Your footsteps.

It is a testimony to the dance,
Of fate and our hearts indeed,
That You simply melded me to You.

There never was a warning,
Never a caress or a whisper,
That could prepare me for You.

I like to think it was You,

And fate making sure,
That I had no way out of bliss.

But my Love, little do You know,
I quite enjoy these traps of fate,
You lay for me when I have lost,
All of me,
Happily,
To You…

His Voice

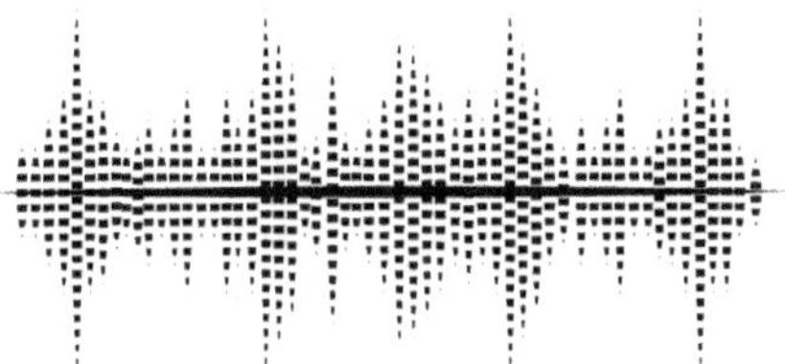

Visions bestowed on me by Time,
Unbelievably paled in the lush face,
Of Your voice that bespoke true prosperity.

Like a huge tongue rough with love,
It slowly snatched my feeble feathers,
Leaving me blissfully bare to You.

Every syllable, every mundane word,
Was my damnation to the unknown,
Recesses of me trembling with insanity.

It held my heart for Your taking,
Sojourned with my soul gracefully,
Self-assuredly tied me to You thusly.

My name now no longer mine,
You owned it within Your feral chords,
Holding me where none have ever been.

I have since been mesmerised,
By You like I have never been,
A rich dark magic that clutches all of my being.

So never ever stop serenading me, my Love,
O never You stop poisoning me slowly,
With the wildness growling in Your throaty
beauty…

His Gaze

Penetrated softly by piercing eyes,
So potent that I do not have to see.

Your eyes leave trails burning,
Bleeding away my errant flesh.

They leave the me, who is far more,
Adventurous and courageous to conquer,
Not only skies but all the seas.

Finally seeing the world through You,
I see it as a garden brimming,
With all the love my old eyes,
Could never contain nor ever see.

No wonder You came and stopped,
By my side, Your songs are,
After all silent laments all for me,
To etch Your very words onto You…

Terrifying love

Maybe I was terrified,
Blessed by a thunderbolt of,
A wave, delightfully knocking me,
Around all that I knew then.

Never could I comprehend it,
As moments after I was enveloped,
In Your love, staving my pain,
Through Your omniscience and omnipresence.

How could I let an enervated heart,
Blemish You who defies all,
Be it divinity or humanity,
So I ripped it out at last.

Facing this gentle harp of mine,
Led me to play strains unknown,
So all strings could be ready,
To douse me in Your scalding scent.

In defiance of life and death,
These songs tell me, O Love,
That it is Your love for me,
Making my harp heart love me finally…

Ferocious

Born from flames,
Clothed in zephyrs,
Breathing underwater,
I have never known earth.

So I burn on and on,
Doused cheerfully in storms,
Building castles of gales,
Where all my creations regale.

For You I shall let loose,
All my ferocity at once,
Letting You rejoice aplenty,
In the shower of Your ichor.

Return those bouquets with,
Your piquant stings in them,
So I too can roar heartily,
With the pain only You can give me…

Painted in Your pain

There are types of pain,
That I want only from You.

Maybe that's why,
I am strong,
To keep my skin clean,
For Your searing paints.

And that's why
I am forgetful,
To keep my mind clean,
For all Your memories.

All so that I can,
Douse myself in You,
Wholly,
Unforgivably,
Irreversibly.

Lit by the flames,
Of pasts gone by,
And imperfect futures,
Without You.

Pulled into paradise

So as to not sully,
This nascent being of mine,
I could never truly see,
The demise of deceased worlds.

All You allow me to see,
Are lights residing in our dark,
Recesses, of our playful spirits,
Ever ready to pounce on us.

Indeed, this is paradise,
After all, does it not speak,
To the deepest desires of ours,
In languages of our hands?

It is special only to us,
A home right in the midst,
Of volatile deserts shifting,
Restlessly, for a morsel of our chaos.

It is here, I see, that,
I shall die and be born,
Aplenty, till I have reached,
The pinnacle of my soul,
Through You…

Breaking down

Weaving away my desires,
With twines soft as light,
They are my hopes,
Set on the tapestry of my skin.

Dare I say they are the best?
Many have glanced back,
Hankering for more,
Luxuriating in its fiery calm.

None have caught my eye,
A body worthy to wear my skin,
A heart deep enough to be my earth,
A voice strong enough to stop me.

Days and years I have,
Waited, dreamt, cried in the cold,
With Time stealing my warmth,
And seasons baring me to naked fires.

Burnt and cold, I saw You,
My skin in tatters and heart silent,
As I realise how Love broke me,
Only to bring me to You.

Quiet wish or two

Oceanic sunsets caught my eye,
I want to see myself through Your eyes,
A painter of such divine riches,
Capturing the muse in His canvas fingers.

Your animalian serenades shook my soul,
Where I always want to hear my name,
A hellion of untold enigma,
Gracing the tardy world with His singing skin.

Your poetic myths seal the void in me,
Their folds I forever want to clothe me,
A solitary bard taming tempestuous seas and me,
Garnishing scorched souls with His scalding
colours.

So, is it too much to ask for,
Is it a wish made too many,
Would You ever let me immerse,
In Your artistry for eternity?

Tell me, O Love of mine, my heart,
Would you care to grace my gardens,
With Your heart of a home?

So close to me

Your sonorous greetings,
Your lips caressing my name,
Why does it feel so familiar,
Yet like nowhere I have ever been?

Writhing in vice-like grips,
Of lonely nights cold with tears,
Why does Your warmth feel,
Like my long-lost home to me?

I was prepared to burn away,
The world with my searching feet,
I am awestruck to see now,
My destiny has been right next to me.

I was going to let ages flow by,
Searching for my heart's solace,
How could I have ever imagined,
That my soul's lullabies wear Your face?

Forgive me, my Love, I have wronged
You, by flying so nobody could
Reach my feet faster than thoughts,
That nobody's arms could ever breach.

Will You find it in You, O Love,
To forgive me in Your arms,
So our nights can finally,
Breathe the lights they need?

Many hearts

Indeed,
What a hapless blessing!
My little heart cannot,
Contain You.

So I have begun entreating,
My soul, to give me many more,
To hold my love for You,
In them, safe from throngs.

I have begun to lose,
My breath and my peace,
So I beg my body to give me,
Many hearts as love's amnesty.

These hearts will surely,
Hold my fires of all-consuming,
Love, staving off death,
From a world up in love's flames.

Rather than You, I realise now,
It is I who would be miserable,
For I am looking at death,
In the face of our immortality.

So many hearts are what we need,
To keep on being free…

Snakes

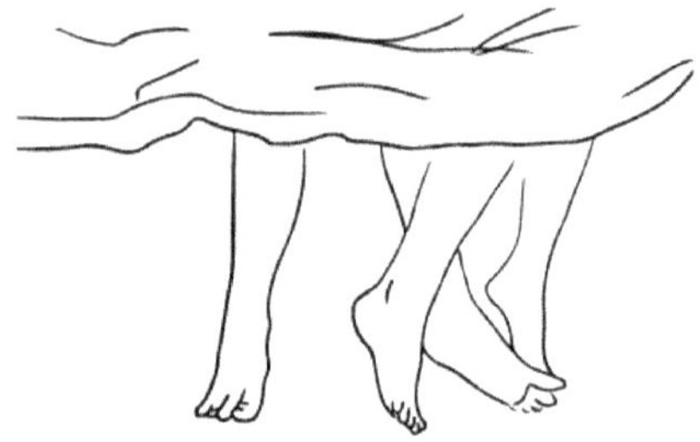

Along my spine,
In the pit of my being,
A humongous serpent unfurls,
With its dark hood gleaming.

My blood has turned,
To its sibilant acolytes,
As they ride on my flames,
Swathing me in a new way.

Floating in the lap of,
A million bites and tongues,
Both flaming and caressing,
This fire is new to the fire in me.

Coiled in their swaying,
Dances, my eyes seek You,
In a swirling mass of venom and,
Waves, singing You, feeling You…

Blood Calls

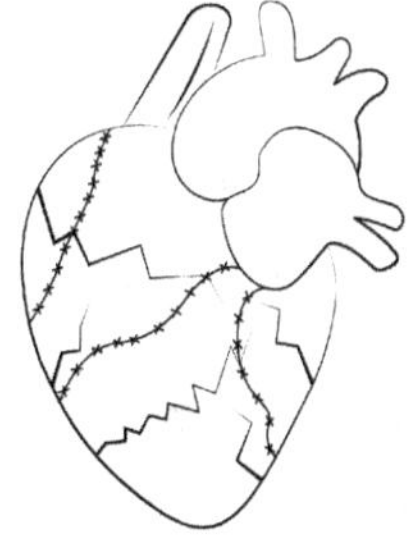

Your growling blood,
Calls out to mine in whispers,
Left on our precipice,
In sweet splatters.

Your blood sings to me,
In a tongue I yet am,
To grasp with and taste on,
My tastebuds.

Familiar tastes of my
Unfamiliarity are perhaps,
An echo from the chambers,
In my blood running.

That is why I continually fail,
Perhaps, in distinguishing us,
Blood from blood,
Teary pasts from our sweet future.

At Peace

Panting under the venom,
Emboldening my dolorous frame,
Gratefully I look up to stars,
That gave their moon a veil.

Peace could thus prance,
Untrammelled by any prying eyes,
Fought for over infinite lifetimes,
Or a few chance moments?

Us broken children in our world,
Draw its breath, languorously,
Hardened by the iron of blood,
Softened by swords of rocky paths.

Peace can thrive in thunderstorms,
Provided we faithfully let down,
Our guards to our skins,
Anointed by our world's deities in rains.

Then it shall matter not,
If we are grievously hurt,
Broken walls are, after all,
Where peace shall always find us…

Defiance

A heady concoction greets me,
My nose and my mind as,
I enter the chaos anew.

My ears are filled by,
Jubilant queries about,
Submitting to Time.

Reflecting on the daze,
A while passes as my heart,
Stirs to mutiny.

A world I got after losing,
Myself and all that was mine,
I will fight Time to keep it.

There shall never be sense,
No false beds of assurances,
I will break the world for my storms.

Homes are an absurdity here,
In a world of mere blinks,
I hereby defy life as I claim it,

For me and You…

Unbound

While freeing You and me,
From the bindings of,
Puny Time and sanity,
Allow me to break the world.

Buried beneath its veneered
Reality, lies my little heart,
Hanging onto each of its pulse,
Now eager to beat to Your rhythm.

Among its crumbling apologies,
This world has nothing more,
So please let me build You,
A house made of coincidences.

All that You can possibly,
Desire and dream about,
It is already Yours because,
At Your feet lies our rationality.

So, my Love, tread dauntlessly,
For my hands will hold You,
Should the green snakes hiss,
Disapproval tipped with incredulity,
At Your handcrafted destiny…

New Era

It is the hour of morn,
Steeped in realisation,
Tasting my incredulity,
And calling out my dubiety.

It really is the start,
Of a new day or is it,
A new life, meant to be spent,
Harvesting the glorious sunshine.

I never realised I could,
Paint with its new colours,
They are the known devils,
For my heart's alacrity.

Never have I seen,
These flowers of unmatched sheen,
Maybe I shall fill my gardens,
With their smiles to remind me.

That the hour of sleep is gone,
The pathos of blurred reality,
Shattered, on the doorstep of,
My soul's hunger for discoveries…

Fire and Water

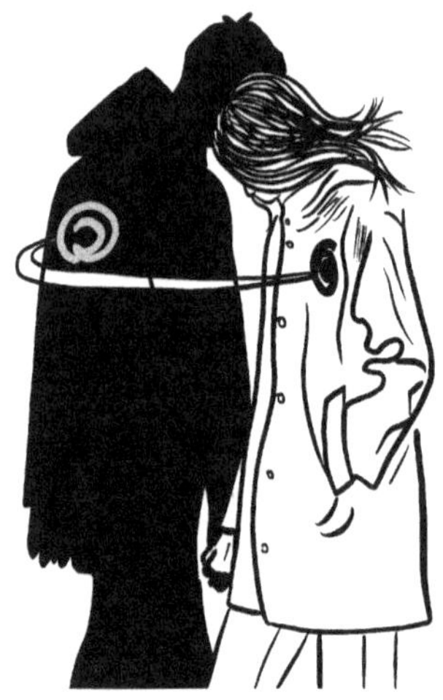

Mists are what I always wake to,
Now that I am finally with You.

There is a new heat enveloping,
Perhaps it rides on waves of frost.

I wonder where my anxiety,
And fearsome troughs go.

It is as if I have found,
A corner deep within me.

It thrums with adamant tenacity,
A certainty that has never before touched me.

Like a humongous fire encapsulated,
In the limitless arms of the ocean's love.

That is what others shall see,
My unstoppable flames in Your immovable seas.

A perfect balance of wills,
A sweet dance of harmony…

My Morning

At last I found You.

The fire creeping at the edges,
Of my nights and dusks,
A blinding masterpiece,
I call my morning.

Turgid turbidity sable,
Slashed incredibly by strokes,
Of a paintbrush melting,
My tepid fires to suns.

Indeed I am favoured,
For I have not dissolved,
In the downpour of dew,
And countless suns smiling at me.

I see I lost myself,
On the bloodied precipice,
To dive into the morning residing,
In the ocean bed awaiting me.

I had to walk the night,
Away, to its obvious oblivion,
So I can embrace You,
In my vigour and anticipation.

Life together

From being my morning,
My mornings are with You,
From dreaming away nights,
My nights have been in You.

A dance of smoke and sea spray,
Often melded on water and fire,
Such a life together of ours,
Would shatter realities in dualities.

My hellfires find solace in You,
Your endless depths are contained in me,
So why would our world ever need,
Any form or voice to be heard or seen?

Sometimes geysers would greet me,
While You shall be showered in steam,
But come what may, my Love,
There can be no end to our chase.

To forge our heart's desire in steel,
To contain the absurdity of divinity,
In our watery fires,
In our fiery waters…

Only You

Just because my restless heart,
Houses Your essence carefully,
That is why my fiery being is at peace,
In the worldly bosom of the mighty seas.

Wherever my dancing feet take me,
A part of You meets me surely,
As if waiting hidden away in crevices,
Of my consciousness, to hold me.

It is the decadent breathing,
That never truly leaves my side,
While my mind stretches its arms,
Wide, to capture every world.

It is the certainty that You are,
In every morsel of a delicious world,
The potential brewing in my feelings,
Perfuming all that I create and touch.

Apparently it is You, only You,
Who else can juggle worlds effortlessly,
When even titans break their backs,
Your visage breaks only in smug smiles.

Yes,
It can only ever be You…